From:

To: Aaron Michael Tate

Thank You,

Love Your
Mother, Angela
April 2014

"Aly"

Everlasting Love

Everlasting Love

Devotions and Meditations
on God's Love for You:
A 31-day Devotional Journal

Patricia King and Robert Hotchkin

© 2012 Patricia King and Robert Hotchkin

All Rights Reserved. No part of this publication may be reproduced, stored in a retrieval system or transmitted in any form or by any means – electronic, mechanical, photocopy, recording or any other – except for brief quotations in printed reviews, without the prior permission of the author.

Unless otherwise identified, Scripture quotations are taken from the NEW AMERICAN STANDARD BIBLE®, Copyright © 1960,1962,1963,1968, 1971,1972,1973,1975,1977,1995 by The Lockman Foundation. Used by permission.

Scripture quotations marked (NKJV) have been taken from the New King James Version. Copyright © 1982 by Thomas Nelson, Inc. Used by permission. All rights reserved.

Scripture quotations marked (NLT) are taken from the Holy Bible, New Living Translation, copyright © 1996, 2004, 2007 by Tyndale House Foundation. Used by permission of Tyndale House Publishers, Inc., Carol Stream, Illinois 60188. All rights reserved.

Scripture quotations marked (WEB) are taken from the World English Bible, public domain.

Published by XP Publishing
PO Box 1017
Maricopa, Arizona 85139
www.XPpublishing.com

ISBN: 978-1-62166067-5

Printed in the United States of America.
For Worldwide distribution

"I have loved you with
an everlasting love;
Therefore I have drawn you
with lovingkindness."

–Jeremiah 31:3–

Dedicated:

To those
who are hungry
to know His love.

Contents

Day 1 13

Day 2 15

Day 3 17

Day 4 19

Day 5 21

Day 6 23

Day 7 25

Day 8 27

Day 9 29

Day 10 31

Day 11 33

Day 12 35

Day 13 37

Day 14 39

Day 15 41

Day 16 43

Day 17 45

Day 18 47

Day 19 49

Day 20 51

Day 21 53

Day 22 55

Day 23 57

Day 24 59

Day 25 61

Day 26 63

Day 27 65

Day 28 67

Day 29 69

Day 30 71

Day 31 73

My Journal of Love Insights 75

Appendix:
How to Have a Fruitful Devotional Time 103

Daily Devotions

Day 1

"I HAVE LOVED YOU WITH AN EVERLASTING LOVE;
THEREFORE I HAVE DRAWN YOU WITH LOVINGKINDNESS."
—JEREMIAH 31:3—

God's love is so marvelous – perfect and flawless. Once you fully believe in and receive His love, it will transform you. God created you with a need for love; it is your deepest and greatest need.

The yearning for God's love is so deep-seated and primal, we can recognize that something vital is missing but not know what it is. The drive to meet this need influences our relationships and much more. You are the focus of God's deepest affection. As soon as you discover His love and allow it to fill you, your core becomes stronger; your relationships and other areas in your life fall into divine order.

When Father God looks at you, His heart is flooded with delight, and He desires you to understand … believe in … and experience His beautiful gift of love. He has specially designed moments so He can reveal His love to you every day. Look for them. He is constantly drawing you to Himself with lovingkindness.

Many times we mistake His gifts of love as merely "good fortune." However, when you examine them you will discover that your adoring Father was the origin of "every good and perfect gift" (James 1:17) that you have ever experienced.

Drink deeply of His love. Focus on His love. Believe in His love.

HE LOVES YOU WITH AN EVERLASTING LOVE…
HE REALLY DOES!

–Patricia King

Day 2

"For God loved the world so much that He gave His one and only Son, so that everyone who believes in Him will not perish but have eternal life."
—John 3:16 NLT—

What Jesus did for us at the Cross is the most powerful thing to ever happen in all of history. God manifested Himself as a man, came to earth to live a perfect life on our behalf, and then went to the Cross to pay the penalty so that all sin for all time and all people could be forgiven. Truly astounding!

As Christians, we are sometimes so understandably overwhelmed by *what* Jesus did at the Cross that we may miss the profoundly simple truth of *why* He did it – LOVE!

The *what* of the Cross is forgiveness of sin. The *why* of the Cross is love. Jesus did the amazing thing that He did so that you would know this amazing truth – YOU ARE LOVED! Meditate on that for a moment.

Jesus did all that He did in the earth and at the Cross for one simple reason. He loves you. He is so completely, totally, and utterly in love with you that He came to die on the Cross to restore you to holiness in Him, so that He could be restored to relationship with you. That is how in love with you He is. That is how deeply, fully, and overwhelmingly loved you are.

Yes, God loves the world. Yes, God loves everyone. Yes, He loves the church, and He loves the sinner. That's all true. But here is the message of the Cross, the most profound revelation in all of Christianity, and it may well be the most important thing you will ever hear: God loves YOU!

The Cross declares throughout all time – in a voice louder than any lie of the enemy or chatter of tribulation in your life – the truth that you are loved. Look to the Cross today. Celebrate *what* Jesus did for you, and rejoice over *why* He did it!

THE MESSAGE OF THE CROSS IS *YOU ARE LOVED!*

–Robert Hotchkin

Day 3

"SEE HOW GREAT A LOVE THE FATHER HAS BESTOWED ON US, THAT WE WOULD BE CALLED CHILDREN OF GOD; AND SUCH WE ARE."
—1 JOHN 3:1—

Your Heavenly Father loves you with a perfect love. You are His own dear child whom He longed for before establishing the foundations of the world. Regardless of your parents' intentions, or lack of them, you are not in any way a mistake. You were specially created by Him with unique qualities and for a particular purpose. You were fashioned by His love for His love, and you continuously fill His thoughts – you are adored!

I had the blessing of being in the delivery room when my grandson was born. All during his time in the womb, my love for him grew. The morning of his birth, I was filled with so much elation and joy – I cannot convey it in words. As a newly born infant, he had not accomplished anything special to deserve my love … or given me any gifts … or even paid me any attention. He had done nothing to warrant such deep feelings of love, and yet I had never experienced anything so deeply moving. The joy of his presence filled every part of my being.

When I considered this, Father spoke to my heart and said, "This is just a glimpse of the kind of love I have for you." At that moment, I understood as never before the depth of God's love, and I broke into tears. Oh, such love!

My grandson is older now and, like every child, he has his "moments" that aggravate me; however, nothing can make me feel any different toward him. I love him – oh, how I love him!

Ponder the perfect, relentless love the Father has for you. Nothing you do or fail to do can make Him withdraw it. He will always love you … with an everlasting love!

OH, BEHOLD, WHAT MANNER OF LOVE IS THIS?

–Patricia King

Day 4

"You can be sure I have seen the misery of My people ...
I am aware of their suffering.
I have come to rescue them."
—Exodus 3:7-8 NLT—

God knows everything we are going through. He also knows that when we are in the midst of a trial, especially a prolonged one, it can seem like He isn't there or that He doesn't care. But that is not true. God is always with us. He is always working on our behalf. And He always has a glorious plan to rescue us from the oppressions of the enemy and bring us into the blessings of victory. We begin to enter into that place as soon as we choose to trust His love and goodness in the midst of our current circumstances, letting go of any discouragement or despair that may have hardened our heart toward Him.

The Lord will never violate our free will. If we have hardened our hearts toward Him, choosing not to believe His heart toward us, we cannot receive from Him. The only thing that can block His love, His promises, and His blessings from our lives is us. That is why He loves to remind us of how much He cares for us. Nothing softens a hardened heart like love!

Look at how the Lord reached out to Moses in Exodus 3:7-8. The first thing the Lord did was assure Moses that He was aware of everything the Israelites had been going through. No matter how it might have seemed or felt all those years, He had not abandoned them. He cared deeply for them, and He was going to rescue them. Moses chose to believe in and trust the lovingkindness of God. That began the process of all the Israelites being set free.

Isn't it amazing that it only took one person believing in the goodness of God to shift things in the lives of the people and the nation of Israel?

Are you going through a difficult time? Does it feel like it may never end? You can begin to shift things today, right now, by looking beyond your circumstances and choosing to believe that God is good. Believe that He cares, He is with you, and He will rescue you. You will not only shift things for yourself but, like Moses, you just might shift things for your entire nation.

> NO MATTER WHAT YOU ARE GOING THROUGH, GOD WANTS YOU TO KNOW THAT HE CARES, AND THAT HE HAS A PLAN TO RESCUE YOU!

–Robert Hotchkin

Day 5

"How precious also are Your thoughts to me, O God! How vast is the sum of them! If I should count them, they would outnumber the sand."
—Psalm 139:17-18—

When you are in love with someone, you think about them often … day and night! You may have met individuals smitten by love, or remember being one yourself. It is hard for them to focus on anything but the person they love. When they go to sleep, they think of them; when they awake, they are still thinking of them, and they seem to glow. They are oblivious to any flaws or imperfections. They live in a dreamlike state, captivated by the one they love.

This is the very same way God loves you. In Psalm 139, the psalmist describes how God is intimately acquainted with all his ways (you might want to read the entire psalm). Then he comes to realize that God loves him so much He thinks about him continually.

This verse also says God's thoughts toward him are "precious." God's thoughts about you are also precious – every single one of them. His feelings of love cause Him to revel in positive, affirming, and precious thoughts about you.

Those thoughts are too numerous to count, so countless they outnumber the sands of the sea.

> GOD IS COMPLETELY IN LOVE WITH YOU…
> YOU HAVE CAPTURED HIS HEART!
>
> –Patricia King

Day 6

"Just tell them, 'I am...'"
—Exodus 3:14 NLT—

In Exodus 3:14-15, Moses had an amazing conversation with the Lord. God had just told Moses that He was going to deliver the Israelites from all their tests and trials, bringing them out of every bondage and into the plenty of His promises. Moses believed the Lord, but he was not sure the Israelites would. He basically said to God, "This is amazing, Lord, but after all the Israelites have been through, when I tell them what you are about to do, they may not believe me. What should I say to them?" The Lord's answer was, "Just tell them, 'I AM.'"

God doesn't mind our questions. He didn't give up on the Israelites or turn away from them when they had doubts. He simply encouraged them that He was the answer to all their questions. It is the same for us today. He doesn't mind that we have questions; He simply wants us to realize that knowing Him and trusting in His love is the answer that will quiet every fear, every doubt, and every concern.

God, I have been sick for so long; are You really healing me? "I AM!"

God, I seem to be stuck in lack; are You really my provider? "I AM!"

God, this ordeal just won't seem to end; are You really delivering me? "I AM!"

God, everyone has always disappointed me; are You really trustworthy? "I AM!"

God, nothing seems to be working out; are You really bringing me into my hope and destiny? "I AM!"

If you have been enduring and persisting in a faith battle… If fear or doubt has been popping into your mind… If you have ever cried out in discouragement, "God, this is not going the way I thought it would; are you truly working on my behalf?" His answer to you is the same answer He gave to Moses – "I AM!"

GOD DOESN'T MIND YOUR QUESTIONS. HE JUST WANTS YOU TO KNOW THAT HE IS THE ANSWER TO ALL OF THEM.

–Robert Hotchkin

Day 7

"For the Father Himself loves you."
—John 16:27—

I once heard the story of a man who struggled to believe that the Father loved him, since he was always making mistakes and failing in his walk before the Lord.

His counselor explained, "The Father loves you in the same way He loves His Son, Jesus Christ." The man responded, "But the Son is perfect." The counselor replied, "Don't you understand? The Father doesn't love the Son because He is perfect or for what He accomplished – He loves Jesus because He is His Son!" The man broke down in tears. He thought God had a performance-based approval system, so he had tried to make himself pleasing to God to gain his love, but he had always failed. Self-condemnation ruled him, resulting in an "orphan spirit." That day, he realized his sonship was based solely on God's love, and it transformed his life.

Do you think there is anything a human being could do well enough or long enough to draw the attention of the God who created the universe? There are over seven billion people living on planet earth – surely some of them are better and more talented than you. Even if you succeeded in gaining God's attention, what could you do that would impress Him enough to make Him love you if He didn't already?

Have you been striving to deserve God's love? Do you truly believe your Heavenly Daddy loves you beyond anything you can imagine – not because you deserve it but because you are His very own? He longed for a relationship with you so much He sent His Son to a painful death to bear your sins so you could be reconciled to Him as a son or daughter. Then when you accepted salvation, He placed you in the same category as His Son; you are "in Christ." As the Father loves Jesus, so He also loves you. You, too, are His child.

RUN TO DADDY'S ARMS RIGHT NOW. YOU ARE HIS BELOVED CHILD IN WHOM HE DELIGHTS.

–Patricia King

Day 8

"Peter said, 'Man, I do not know what you are saying!' Immediately, while he was still speaking, the rooster crowed. And the Lord turned and looked at Peter."
—Luke 22:60-61 NKJV—

Even in times when we are at our weakest and worst, the Lord wants us to know that He loves us and is there for us. When we are most broken, and in the midst of our greatest failures, God's love for us does not change. His desire is to meet us in those moments, lift us up, and help us move beyond our shortcomings into greater wholeness through a greater revelation of His love.

In Luke 22:60, Peter was at his lowest moment. He had given in to fear and denied Jesus three times, exactly as the Lord said he would (Luke 22:31-34). Scripture tells us that at that very moment Jesus "turned and looked at Peter." I don't believe Jesus turned His face to Peter with a look of hurt or disappointment or to say, "Seriously?! After all I have done for you? You couldn't stand with Me, you couldn't stick up for Me? You denied Me?" No. I believe that Jesus turned His face to Peter in that moment to let him know that He was right there with him, that He loved him no matter what, and that His love for him would not ever change.

This is powerful, but it has even more impact when we look at it in relation to a passage in Numbers 6 where the Lord outlined the Nazirite vow, inviting His people to set themselves apart and walk with Him in a special and committed way. In this context of the people being fully pleasing and committed to Him, the Lord told Moses to have the high priest pronounce His greatest blessing over the Israelites – that He would turn His face to them and shine His countenance upon them.

In Luke 22:61 when Peter had just denied Jesus three times, what did the Lord do? He turned His face to Peter! He shone His countenance upon him! He released the great blessing of Numbers 6:22-24 to Peter even though he had just failed miserably at being fully committed to the Lord. This is the good news of Jesus Christ! His love for us, and His blessings to us, are not based on what we do but on who He is! Even in our worst moments and greatest failings, the Lord wants us to know He loves us and is there for us. At our most broken, all God wants is for us to turn toward Him so we will realize He never turns away from us.

God's love for you is not based on what you do; it is based on who He is!

–Robert Hotchkin

Day 9

> "THROWING ASIDE HIS CLOAK, HE JUMPED UP
> AND CAME TO JESUS."
> —MARK 10:50—

This Scripture reveals a drastic change of identity for a blind man named Bartimaeus. In those days, people with health conditions that hindered them from working were given a "cloak" by the government. This permitted them to legally receive alms, and people could give knowing there was a legitimate need. His cloak identified Bartimaeus officially as a blind beggar.

Bartimaeus had heard about Jesus' compassion for the suffering and how He healed them. Bartimaeus' faith arose for healing. When Jesus came to his region, Bartimaeus was determined to press in for his healing; he shouted loudly, "Jesus, Son of David, have mercy on me!" (Mark 10:47). Even though many told him to be silent, he refused because He trusted in the love of Jesus.

Jesus stopped when He heard that cry of faith and said, "Call him here" (verse 49). He was filled with love and compassion for this desperate man who captivated His attention.

When Bartimaeus understood Jesus was calling for him, he threw off his cloak. This was a massive act of faith! Throwing aside the cloak meant he was leaving behind his identity as a blind beggar and abandoning his means for making a living. Bartimaeus, however, let it all go because he was convinced of the love and mercy of Jesus. Bartimaeus had 100% faith in Jesus' ability and desire to heal him.

That day Bartimaeus got his new identity. He cast off the old description of "blind beggar" and received perfect vision. Now free from his disability, he became a passionate follower of Jesus.

Jesus also wants you to be free, in every area of your life. Do you wear a "cloak" that binds you to a mistaken identity? For example, do you think of yourself not as a person with an addiction to alcohol but as an alcoholic? Take courage, toss it aside, and allow Christ's love to clothe you with a new identity.

THROW ASIDE MISTAKEN, LIMITING BELIEFS OF WHO YOU ARE BECAUSE OF WHAT YOU'VE DONE, AND RECEIVE A NEW IDENTITY BASED ON CHRIST'S LOVE.

–Patricia King

Day 10

"GOD IS LOVE."
—1 JOHN 4:8 NLT—

In his gospel and throughout his epistles, John often wrote about the love of God. But in 1 John 4:8 the Apostle of Love made an even more powerful statement than, "God loves us." He declared: God *is* love. When we catch the subtle but powerful impact of this statement, it sets us free from ever having to wonder if God really does love us – or if we truly deserve to be so radically and perfectly loved by Him. When we understand what the apostle John understood, we never worry again about having to earn God's love, because the love of God simply *is*.

When we realize that God is love, we step into an unshakeable certainty that God loves us. Why? Because we come to understand that God does not choose to love us, He is love. So we never have to be concerned that He might choose not to love us. God cannot not love. He *is* love. So it is impossible for Him who is love to not love. Do you see it? God loves you because He is love. Love is not what God does. It is who He is. You cannot cause God to stop loving you, because you cannot cause God to stop being God!

Now let's take this one step further. Why does God save? Because He loves – John 3:16 makes this clear. It is the same for all of God's blessings and promises. He saves because He loves. He heals because He loves. He delivers because He loves. He provides because He loves. He protects because He loves. He revives, renews, refreshes, and restores because He loves. And He loves, not because He chooses to or we deserve it, but because He *is* love.

Just as we can be certain of God's love for us, we can be certain of His healing, deliverance, provision, and all of His other blessings and benefits. It's not because of who we are or what we do. It is because of who God is – our amazing Jesus who not only loves us, but who *is* love.

YOU ARE LOVED. AND YOU CAN BE CERTAIN OF IT, BECAUSE GOD IS LOVE.

–Robert Hotchkin

Day 11

"And some men were carrying on a bed a man who was paralyzed; and they were trying to bring him in and to set him down in front of Him."
—Luke 5:18—

There is nothing like the love of a friend! In Luke 5, we find a paralyzed man with friends who truly loved him. We are not sure how long the paralyzed man had been in this condition or how long his friends had known him, but we see love in action. They heard that Jesus healed the sick and they were determined to help their friend.

They did for their friend what he could not do for himself. They carried him on his bed to the meeting hall. By the time they arrived, they were disappointed to find the hall too full to enter. However, love is persistent. They carried him up to the roof, which I'm sure was no easy task. Love is a compelling force that enables us to face difficulties and break through any resistance. These faithful friends not only had the struggle of getting their buddy on the roof but they made a hole in it and lowered him directly in front of Jesus. They positioned their friend where Jesus could not miss him.

Neither could Jesus have missed their faith. He told the paralytic his sins were forgiven. That's something to think about. The paralytic's friends probably knew he had "issues," but true love looks beyond human flaws.

The paralytic received both forgiveness and healing that day, because he had friends who loved him. Do you have friends who love you like that? If so, thank the Lord for them; they are treasures in your life. Perhaps you could drop them a note of thanks and appreciation.

Finally, are you such a friend to others? Look for opportunities to activate your love and faith to help those in need … be a true friend.

THE LOVE OF A FRIEND
IS ONE OF THE GREATEST GIFTS IN LIFE!

–Patricia King

Day 12

"The beloved of the Lord shall dwell in safety."
—Deuteronomy 33:12 NKJV—

The word *beloved* is one of God's favorites. In some Bible translations, He uses it more than one hundred times. It is how He thinks of you. You are His beloved.

Beloved is more than just a name the Lord has given you, or a term of endearment He calls you. It is also your job description – you were created to *be loved*!

If you have ever wondered why God brought you forth, it is simple. You were created by Him to receive, know, and experience His love. That is why you are on the earth.

When you find yourself in a difficult situation and wonder what the Lord would have you do to triumph, remember your job description. He wants you to be loved, beloved. He wants you to know and receive His love so that in all situations and circumstances, instead of being overcome with fear or doubt or confusion, you will remember and experience how fully and completely He cares for you and watches over you. He wants you to be loved, beloved. Because as you believe that love and receive that love, you will remember that you have not been given a spirit of fear but one of love, empowering you to refuse anxiety and cast aside doubt and confusion (2 Timothy 1:7). He wants you to be loved, beloved. Because His love for you contains and guarantees all of His promises to you.

The next time the devil tries to use the news of the day, or a doctor's report, or your bank statement to create anxiety in you, don't receive it. Instead, take a moment to remember that you are God's beloved. Take a moment to be loved by Him. As you receive His love, all fear will go (1 John 4:18) and your soul will once again focus on Him and His love for you. Rest in His love. And know that no matter what temporary facts might seem to say, the eternal truth is that God loves you and He is well able to perform His Word in your life.

YOU ARE THE BELOVED OF GOD.
YOU WERE CREATED TO BE LOVED!

–Robert Hotchkin

Day 13

"Jesus said to him, 'Get up, pick up your pallet and walk.' Immediately the man became well, and picked up his pallet and began to walk."
—John 5:8-9—

Love does not always cater to everyone's needs. In fact, sometimes if we do too much for someone, we are hindering them from receiving the better thing the Lord has for them.

In the situation with the man at the pool of Bethesda, we discover that he had lived with a chronic condition for over 38 years. Jesus asked him, "Do you wish to get well?" (John 5:6) The sick man's answer was unusual. It was not a response to the question but excuses for why he was unable to get into the healing waters in time to receive a healing.

In this situation, Jesus did not pray for the man's healing or even extend a helping hand to draw him to his feet. He simply commanded the suffering man to do something. Jesus ordered, "GET UP! Pick up your bed and start walking."

To some, this might appear to be unsympathetic and uncaring. Had it been you or me, we may have thought, "This man has been sick so long. Shouldn't I help him up?" However, in this case, that would have been a mistake. The most loving act was to call this man out of his "victim mindset" and challenge him to rise up through his own efforts into wholeness!

I once had friends who had financial needs. I had helped them out previously but on one occasion the Lord said, "Tell them they can activate their faith and take action to receive provisions." It was hard for me not to give in to my desire to solve their problem, but I obeyed the Lord. Sure enough, they arose to the occasion and God met their need.

Love always desires the best for another, but if our actions enable a victim mindset, we aren't helping but hindering them. Sometimes the best thing is to hold back and encourage them to soar with their own faith and abilities in the Lord.

Love, Sweet Love!

–Patricia King

Day 14

"Although Jesus loved Martha, Mary, and Lazarus, He stayed where He was for the next two days."
—John 11:5-6 NLT—

Martha, Mary and Lazarus knew the Lord well. He had visited them many times. Martha had cooked for Him and served Him. Mary had sat adoringly at His feet. Lazarus had shared many conversations with Him. They were friends. And even more than that, they believed that Jesus loved them. After all, when Lazarus became seriously ill, the word they sent to Jesus was, "Lord, the one You love is sick."

Martha and Mary were confident enough in the love of Jesus to cry out to Him for help, but then when He did not respond the way they thought He should, it caused them to start questioning that love. To their minds, if He truly cared He would have come right away. They didn't understand why the Lord had not immediately answered when they cried out to Him. They were so upset by this that when Jesus did show up, after Lazarus died, Martha buffeted him with angry questions about why He hadn't responded sooner, and at first Mary couldn't even bring herself to meet with Him (John 11:20-21).

The Lord knew they were confused. He knew they did not understand why He was moving according to God's perfect timing as opposed to their human reasoning. He knew they were upset. He even knew they were questioning if He truly loved them. His response? Simple. He met them exactly where they were and continued to love them and be loving to them. He answered all of Martha's questions and built her back up in her faith (John 11:21-27). He made sure that Mary knew He still very much wanted to see her and spend time with her (John 11:28). And, of course, He resurrected Lazarus, raising him up into fullness of life and health.

Martha and Mary chose to meet with the Lord in the midst of their confusion and questions. They chose to once again trust in His love even though their circumstances had not yet changed. This opened the way for the Lord to move powerfully in their lives – doing exceedingly abundantly beyond what they had originally asked of Him. Their whole community was impacted; everyone in their sphere of influence saw the goodness of God.

There is nothing more powerful than the love of God. And trusting in that love – no matter what – unlocks that power in our lives.

DON'T LET YOUR CIRCUMSTANCES INFLUENCE YOUR REVELATION OF GOD'S LOVE; LET YOUR REVELATION OF GOD'S LOVE INFLUENCE YOUR CIRCUMSTANCES.

–Robert Hotchkin

Day 15

"Immediately Jesus, perceiving in Himself that the power proceeding from Him had gone forth, turned around in the crowd and said, 'Who touched My garments?'"
—Mark 5:30—

The woman with an issue of blood had lived in this terrible condition for over twelve years. She was forbidden by the law of her day to be in public, she was not allowed to touch anyone, and she was labeled UNCLEAN!

In her desperation to find healing, she broke the law. Her faith compelled her to press through the crowd, no doubt making contact with many people before touching the garment of Jesus. Breaking through crowds of people to reach Jesus required much of her strength. As a woman who had been hemorrhaging for twelve years, she was likely frail.

When she grabbed hold of Jesus' garments, she touched more than cloth. She pulled on His gift of miracles with her faith, and Jesus recognized that His power had been released to someone. He asked, "Who touched my garments?"

Jesus' question was more than a request for information; it was an act of love. She had been looked down upon and isolated from society for more than twelve years due to her status. Good folks were not supposed to associate with the likes of her. Jesus took this opportunity to draw attention to her and tell the world that she was changed and now an acceptable person! He not only released healing to her but also restored her to her place in society by freeing her from the law of sin and death. The law that called her "unclean" no longer applied; she was now "healed" of her affliction.

The love of Jesus touches the whole person. He desires that everyone be restored in every way. He was not ashamed to be associated with her in her unclean state, or to be touched by her. Love has no fear … does not care what others think … and makes the unclean clean.

A number of years ago, I was disciplined by the Lord for rejecting a young homeless man who wanted to be around me all the time. On some occasions I purposely avoided him, until one day the Lord spoke to me firmly. He said, "If you continue to reject him, he will become even more unacceptable to you. If you receive him as he is, he will become more acceptable … love him as I love him!" Cut to the core, I repented at once. Soon, I saw the love of God transform him and he became one of our most precious treasures. Love changed him and it changed me, too.

CHRIST'S LOVE DOES NOT REJECT THE "UNCLEAN" BUT ACCEPTS AND RESTORES THEM!

–Patricia King

Day 16

"As the Father has sent Me, I also send you."
—John 20:21 NKJV—

After accomplishing everything He had manifested in the earth to do, Jesus appeared to the disciples and declared an amazing promise to them. He said that just as His Father had sent Him out to impact the world, He was sending them. God's Word is eternal and He is no respecter of persons, so the promise that our risen Lord gave to His disciples in John 20 is for all His disciples for all time – including us!

And what a promise it is – He sends us into the world to share the reality of the Kingdom, just as His Father had sent Him. Amazing! But to lay hold of this promise, we need to understand not just what Jesus was sent to do but *how* He was sent. Because just as He was sent, so are we.

Matthew 3:17, Mark 1:11, and Luke 3:22 reveal how the Father sent Jesus. In these Scriptures we see the Father launch Jesus into His earthly ministry by declaring over Him, "Behold, My beloved Son, in whom I am fully pleased!" The way Jesus was sent was with a declaration of total love and acceptance. He was sent forth to be about His Father's business, knowing He was loved, and that He didn't have to do anything to be worthy of that love. He was adored because He was a Son. Simple as that. But, oh, so important. Jesus confidently moved in all the power He was sent with because He was confident that He was loved and accepted by the One who sent Him.

Before Jesus had done anything on behalf of the Father, before He saved, healed, or delivered anyone, before Jesus had worked a single miracle or resisted one temptation, before He went to the Cross or defeated hell and death, He was certain that He was loved and accepted by the Father. That is how Jesus was sent. In perfect love.

Beloved child of God, that is how you are sent, too. You are sent into every moment and every situation with a declaration that you are loved and God is fully pleased with you. You don't have to earn it. It is yours because you are His! So, go forth into this day and every day knowing you are His beloved child and He is fully pleased with you.

You don't have to do a thing to earn God's love; simply accept that you are His beloved child!

–Robert Hotchkin

Day 17

"Better is open rebuke than love that is concealed."
—Proverbs 27:5—

When I was a young mother, my four-year-old son required discipline. He had been such a good toddler that I honestly had no need to reprimand him until this particular time. One day, I sat him down and explained what he had done wrong and that I had to punish him for his bad behavior. He didn't resist or beg for leniency but instead looked up at me with his big beautiful blue eyes and nodded.

I can't begin to tell you how difficult it was for me to correct him. Later that day, I prayed, "God, discipline me early. I want to fully submit to your discipline like my precious child accepted mine."

Over the years, I have known the faithfulness of the Lord to bring the rebukes, correction, and discipline I needed to keep on the right path. He is so faithful and I love His discipline although it is never comfortable at the moment and is sometimes even painful, but afterwards it has always yielded the "peaceable fruit of righteousness."

A friend once watched as I made mistakes but did not confront me about them. After the mistake caused me to fall flat on my face, she said, "I saw that problem coming months ago, but I was reluctant to say anything."

I would rather have an open criticism than a concealed love that refuses to risk creating an offense. Constructive criticism is uncomfortable for the moment but brings a lifetime of blessing.

> DO NOT DESPISE A FAITHFUL REBUKE
> AND DO NOT CONCEAL YOUR LOVE.

–Patricia King

Day 18

> "'I WANT TO,' HE SAID."
> —MATTHEW 8:3 NLT—

When the leper came to Jesus in Matthew 8, he knew that the Lord *could* heal him, he just wasn't sure that the Lord *would* heal him. The leper was not questioning God's power; he was questioning God's heart.

My favorite version of this conversation is found in the New Living Translation (NLT). Most translations say Jesus' response to the leper was, "I am willing." But in the NLT Jesus said, "I *want* to." I think this much more accurately portrays the incredible heart of our amazing Jesus for the leper, and for every one of us. God is not just *willing* to heal us, and save us, and deliver us, and provide for us, and bless us. He *wants* to. And He wants us to know that He wants to. He loves us, and cares for us, and wants the very best for us. He wants us to know that it is His deepest heart's desire for us to know Him and receive all He has for us.

Those words – "I want to!" – were a revelation to the leper. Society considered him unclean. People ignored and shunned him. He was used to no one wanting to be near him, let alone wanting to bless him. Those words – "I want to!" – revealed the reality of Jesus' heart to the leper. In that moment the leper believed not only in the power of the Lord but in His love. And he was healed!

Whatever you're believing for. Whatever you've been contending for. Take a moment today and remember that the Lord's words to you are the same as they were to the leper. He is able. He is willing. But even more, He *wants* to. He wants to heal you. He wants to deliver you from difficult circumstances. He wants to provide for you, and protect you. It is His deep desire to see you receive and enjoy all of His blessings and all of His promises, for one very simple reason. He loves you. He really, really does.

NOT ONLY CAN YOU TRUST IN GOD'S POWER, YOU CAN TRUST IN HIS HEART!

–Robert Hotchkin

Day 19

"I WILL HEAL THEIR APOSTASY, I WILL LOVE THEM FREELY,
FOR MY ANGER HAS TURNED AWAY FROM THEM."
—HOSEA 14:4—

Many Christians live with guilt, shame, and condemnation due to past failures, sins, and circumstances that alienated them from God during a season of hardship or rebellion.

Consider Peter who walked so close to the Lord and yet in a difficult moment denied Him – not just once but three times. Jesus was so merciful to Peter, as we read in John 21. He reached out to him and restored their relationship and Peter's calling. Jesus gave him a brand new beginning, and the book of Acts tells us Peter became a powerhouse apostle in the early church.

In 1 John 1:9, we find an amazing promise: "If we confess our sins, He is faithful and righteous to forgive us our sins and to cleanse us from all unrighteousness." We serve a righteous, loving, forgiving God!

Hosea tells of the time Israel fell away from the covenant-making, covenant-keeping God. They openly rebelled against Him. Yet, He declared in Hosea 14:4 that He would not turn His anger for their unfaithfulness toward them but away from them. He continued to love them freely and committed to healing their rebellion against Him.

When you sin against yourself, others, and God, it hurts you and everyone your sin touches … even God. He loves you so much He is committed, as He was with Israel, to restore and heal everything that damaged you and others.

Allow Him to remove any guilt, condemnation, or shame from past sin, mistakes, and failures that might be holding you back. God fiercely loves you and wants to heal you. Nothing, not even your biggest mistakes, can separate you from His love. His love is sin-proof!

HE LOVES YOU WITH AN EVERLASTING (INDESTRUCTIBLE) LOVE — HE REALLY DOES!

–Patricia King

Day 20

> "He showed them His hands and His side.
> Then the disciples were glad."
> —John 20:20 NKJV—

In John 20, the disciples were going through a difficult time. They had walked with Jesus for years. They knew the intimacy of His presence. His love and goodness were an everyday occurrence in their lives. They had experienced favor and blessing. They had seen the works of the enemy destroyed at a word. And they had gotten used to walking with Jesus like that.

But now, all of a sudden, things were different. Really different. Jesus had been arrested, tried, and executed. Even though He told them all of this was going to happen, and promised that it would turn out for the best, they had forgotten. All they knew right now was that everything had changed, nothing was going the way they thought it would, and they had no idea what to do. They were scared, confused, and discouraged. So they freaked out and locked themselves away from the world.

That's when Jesus appeared. And what did He do? He showed the disciples His hands and His side. He showed them the wounds He suffered on the Cross. He put on display the evidence of His amazing love for them. When the disciples saw those wounds, when they experienced the tangible reality of the Lord's love for them, everything shifted. Fear bowed, confusion dissipated, and discouragement was destroyed. As the disciples chose to believe the revelation of God's love for them, they were transformed. And so were their circumstances. They went from being imprisoned by fear, to joyfully stepping out in the victory of the finished work of the Cross.

As inescapable as it can seem when we are locked up in doubt, confusion, or despair, there is nothing more powerful than the love of God. So the next time you are in the midst of something difficult, and you catch yourself locked up in fear or discouragement, remember John 20. Remember that Jesus wants to step into your circumstances, just like He did for the disciples, and make His amazing love amazingly real to you.

> TAKE A MOMENT TODAY AND INVITE JESUS TO MAKE HIS LOVE REAL TO YOU!

–Robert Hotchkin

Day 21

"The Lord your God is in your midst, A victorious warrior. He will exult over you with joy,
He will be quiet in His love,
He will rejoice over you with shouts of joy."
—Zephaniah 3:17—

I love the picture this Scripture paints. I see Jesus as a mighty, victorious warrior, happy and rejoicing because He won the battle and obtained His prize, His greatest desire, and most cherished possession – YOU!

He is so excited that He celebrates with loud joyful shouts. Can you hear Him and all of heaven rejoicing with Him? He is screaming with delight, so happy He cannot contain His elation, and must express it!

Have you ever wondered how much God loves you? Yes, YOU? He desired YOU so passionately that He fought and won every battle in order to receive you to Himself. He wrestled through Gethsemane, endured the pain of the Cross, and conquered death and hell. He won! He won and is now eternally ecstatic because you belong to Him.

On the other hand, He is quiet (at rest) in His love for you, because it is settled. Nothing can change or challenge it. He proved His love for you in every way love could be tested. You never need to worry about Him withdrawing His love – His love endures throughout eternity. His love for you is perfect!

Oh, beloved, enter His joy. Gaze upon His perfect, glorious love. You are His and He is yours … forever!

> Behold His love – His heart is full of joy because of you!

–Patricia King

Day 22

"He will be with you,
He will not leave you nor forsake you."
—Deuteronomy 31:8 NKJV—

Over the years I have had some incredible encounters with the Lord – visions, visitations, revelations. I am profoundly grateful for every one of them. But to me, the most wonderful, amazing, loving, and incredible thing about the Lord is that He is *always* there, when I feel Him and when I don't.

God was not more "there" for me during those encounters, visions, and visitations. I was simply more aware of His being there. While I deeply enjoy each and every tangible experience with God that He blesses me with, what I am most grateful for is the certainty that He is always with me. He is always loving me, always guiding and guarding me, always wooing me deeper into all He created me for. And He is doing the same for you – drawing you deeper and deeper into the revelation of His constant presence and certain love.

God has promised that He will never leave you nor forsake you. This means that He is always there for you – the days you feel it, and the days you don't. You are always in His presence, because He is always present. Even His name declares this to you. "I AM" is present tense. It's not "I Was." Not "I Will Be." But, "I AM!" He is a present tense God. Always present, always with you, always there. When you choose to believe this, know it is true, and decide to trust it, you will quickly discover that the Lord is the closest companion and truest friend you could ever have.

Today, instead of waiting for the Lord to "reach down" and touch you, reach out to Him in the certainty of His love, and embrace Him!

> YOU ARE ALWAYS IN GOD'S PRESENCE,
> BECAUSE HE IS ALWAYS PRESENT!

–Robert Hotchkin

Day 23

> "A NEW COMMANDMENT I GIVE TO YOU,
> THAT YOU LOVE ONE ANOTHER, EVEN AS I HAVE LOVED YOU,
> THAT YOU ALSO LOVE ONE ANOTHER."
> —JOHN 13:34—

Jesus modeled perfect love and taught His disciples to love in the same manner.

All of us experience "grace-growers" in our lives, opportunities to learn more about the rich depth of Christ's love.

A number of years ago, I went through a season of heavy persecution and experienced an amazing measure of cruelty from the body of Christ. It was perplexing to me as well as extremely painful at times. I did not understand why the attacks were so vicious. You may have encountered similar things, as few get through life on this planet without facing the cruelty of man's hatred.

However, this season of persecution became one of the greatest blessings of my life because it allowed me to receive a deeper glimpse into the core of Christ's love. He taught me that the "fellowship of His sufferings" mentioned in Philippians 3:10 was a suffering of love.

Scripture teaches that if we do not have love, we are nothing (1 Corinthians 13:2). This is quite the statement; think about it ... no love = no worth. It is easy to love when people are kind and treat you with respect, but love is proven to be authentic when it survives the trials of hatred, cruelty, and mistreatment. Jesus, as always, is our perfect example.

On the Cross, He was abandoned, denied, betrayed, beaten, slandered, lied against, scourged, crowned with thorns, unjustly sentenced, and hung by nails on a tree to die an excruciating, painful, humiliating death. All the while, the crowd chanted, "Crucify Him, crucify Him."

In the middle of all that hate, He not only forgave everyone, but also gave His life for those who hated Him and terribly mistreated Him! We were represented in that sea of unbelieving, hostile humanity. Yet, He took our sin on His shoulders so we could be clothed in His righteousness. He was cursed so we could receive His blessing. He became poor so we could have His riches.

This kind of love is what He invites us to have for one another. Are you ready to say "YES" to this wonderful commandment? There is a cost, yet the reward is beyond anything you can aspire to in this life ... to be like Jesus.

OH, TO BE LIKE HIM!

–Patricia King

Day 24

"WE LOVE HIM BECAUSE HE FIRST LOVED US."
—1 JOHN 4:19 NKJV—

Jesus had a message for the church at Ephesus in Revelation 2:1-5. He was concerned that, in spite of all their good works, the church had forgotten the love they had in the beginning. He then went on to tell them how to correct this, and the remedy was amazingly simple. The Lord instructed the church to remember their "first love." That's it. That's the key to breaking free of the numbing drudgery of works-based religion and re-igniting a fresh heart of burning passion for an ongoing intimate relationship with God.

So, what is this "first love" that is so powerful?

Many think that what Jesus is referring to is the first love we feel when we initially come to know Him. But I don't believe that is what He is getting at. I don't think the Lord is saying that the remedy is for us, in our own strength, to try to stir up our passion for Him. I think the Lord is saying that the key is for us to remember His passion for us, and be stirred by that. 1 John 4:19 says we love Him because He *first loved* us. What the Lord was sharing with the church at Ephesus, and all of us, is that when we need our passion sparked afresh, the key is to take time off from what we are doing *for* Him and simply spend time *with* Him, remembering who He is and how much He loves us.

The "first love" we must always remember is His amazing, incredible, merciful, gracious, glorious, abounding love for us. When we return to that, we are overwhelmed afresh and our love for Him blossoms anew. When we remember His passion for us, we cannot help but be passionate for Him. By returning to our "first love," we are returning to that overwhelming moment that changed everything – and our only response will be to fall completely, totally, and fully in love with Jesus all over again, even more passionately than before!

THE BEST WAY TO IGNITE FRESH PASSION FOR THE LORD IS TO REMEMBER HIS BURNING PASSION FOR YOU!

–Robert Hotchkin

Day 25

"Just as the Father has loved Me, I have also loved you; abide in My love.... for the Father Himself loves you, because you have loved Me and have believed that I came forth from the Father."
—John 15:9, 16:27—

It is easy to believe that the Father loves Jesus. Why wouldn't He? Jesus has perfect love, flawless character, and is an obedient Son.

Looking at ourselves in contrast, we can think, "I'm a believer but I am a failure at love, flawed in character, and I'm not always obedient to the things God asks of me. How can the Father possibly love me like He loves Jesus?"

This is the mystery of God's love. He loves us, because … well, just because He does, and nothing can change it! In addition, He has promised to love us with an "everlasting love" – and that means ever … as in continuously, all the time … lasting! Don't bother trying to understand, just believe it.

Human love is fickle. When a relational challenge hits us, we often give up and throw in the towel. In our society today, few keep their word to each other and many marriage vows are broken within the first five years of marriage.

Spouses leave each other and their children, church members leave their congregations, and friends break their relationships over the slightest disagreements. When Jesus said He loves us as the Father loves Him, He is talking about a love that never fails – no matter what! That's the love we are called to "abide" in. This means He desires for us to live in this excellent, divine, quality of love … and He wouldn't ask it of us if we were unable to do it! Think about that; you may have to upgrade your beliefs about what you are capable of doing.

In order for us to love others as He loves us, we have to first receive His love, abide in His love daily, and examine how perfect His love is towards us. Drink deeply of this perfect love, steep yourself in it, soak it in, and you will be able to share it with others. Choose today to live in this kind of love every waking hour. Make love your greatest aim in life!

> ABIDE IN HIS LOVE – MEDITATE ON HIS LOVE ALL DAY LONG AND REST IN IT ALL NIGHT.

–Patricia King

Day 26

> "GOD SAW ALL THAT HE HAD MADE,
> AND BEHOLD, IT WAS VERY GOOD."
> —GENESIS 1:31—

Each day during the first five days of creation, when the Lord brought something forth He would look upon what He had created and call it "good." But on the sixth day, something special happened. He made man. And when He did, He gazed upon all He had created in man – a son, a companion, a friend, someone for Him to walk with and talk with and spend time with, someone for Him to love, adore, and lavish Himself upon – and He declared that this was not just good, but *very* good.

The word *very* in the original Hebrew is "m'od" and it means "wholly, especially, exceedingly, utterly." Right from the beginning, the Lord declared that we were special to Him, above all else in His heart.

Just as the Lord made Adam, He made you. No matter what the circumstances of your birth were, it was God who formed you in your mother's womb and brought you forth, because He wanted you in this world. He wanted to know you. He wanted you to be His child. He wanted to walk with you and talk with you and spend time with you. He wanted to shine His love upon you. This is why you were created. This is why He brought you into the world.

The words the Lord spoke over Adam when He created him are the same words the Lord spoke over you when He brought you forth, declaring that in His eyes you are *"very good."* To this day, the Lord looks upon you, lights up with love, and declares you are wholly, especially, exceedingly, and utterly good. He adores you – every bit of you. And He wants you to know that you matter to Him, *very* much. On your best days. On your worst days. Every day. The Lord wants you to know that you are His child, and in His eyes you are, and always will be, *very* good.

GOD MADE YOU. GOD LOVES YOU
AND GOD CELEBRATES YOU.

–Robert Hotchkin

Day 27

"But God demonstrates His own love toward us, in that while we were yet sinners, Christ died for us."
—Romans 5:8—

In the gospels, the religious leaders accused Jesus of being a "friend of sinners." He was faulted for hanging out with tax collectors and those living in obvious sin (Matthew 11:19). In that day, the people were expected to separate themselves from filthy sinners, those not living by the standards of their traditions or the law.

Yet we see Jesus consistently reaching out to the marginalized people of society. His love caused Him to break through the barriers of tradition and draw sinful people to repentance. He cared about the woman caught in adultery. After rescuing her from those who had cruelly judged her and intended to stone her, He urged her to "sin no more." He went to the homes of tax collectors (Jewish traitors who collected taxes for Rome), had dinner with sinners, touched "the untouchable" lepers, spoke with ostracized Samaritans, and had a motley crew of disciples and support staff that included a tax collector, a betrayer, and a former adulteress.

Yes, they accused Jesus of associating with sinners, yet that was His very mission. He did not come for the righteous but for the sinners. We need to remind ourselves that without Christ we are all sinners, no matter how respectable we believe we are.

The Bible says, "For all have sinned and fall short of the glory of God" (Romans 3:23). Our self-righteousness is just as wicked as our unrighteousness. The devout Saul killed Christians for what he believed was a noble cause, but Christ died for him, too. Consequently, the self-righteous Saul became Paul, the apostle of grace, because of Christ's love. Jesus loves the religious as well as the unrighteous.

Today, let's love like Jesus, loving both the self-righteous and the unrighteous.

Love them to life!

–Patricia King

Day 28

"Since He did not spare even His own Son but gave Him up for us all, won't He also give us everything else?"
—Romans 8:32 NLT—

Before you ever gave your heart to the Lord, He already had gone to the Cross for you. With no guarantee that you would choose to give yourself to Him, He gave everything for you. He gave the extravagant love gift of the Cross just for the chance that you might one day be His. That's what He thinks of you. That's how much He loves and values you. That is the generosity of His extravagant heart for you.

So, with that in mind, now that you *are* His, now that you have freely given yourself to Him, why would you ever think that He would withhold any good thing from you? If He did everything for you before you said yes to Him, you can be certain that all He is and all He has are yours now that you are His. God gave Himself fully to you at the Cross, not only so you could be restored to relationship with Him but also so you would never have to question or doubt that all He is, all He has, all His Kingdom, all His promises, all His blessings and benefits are also yours. Yes, He wants to have a relationship with you, and just as much, He wants you to have everything He has made available to you in that relationship. It is His great joy to see you enjoying all His blessings and benefits.

When we look at the sacrifice of Jesus and realize how completely the Lord gave Himself for us, it becomes easy to believe that He has also generously given everything to us. We don't have to earn it, or work for it, or wonder if we deserve it – we haven't, we can't, and we don't! He did it all anyway. It is all ours regardless, not because of what we do but because of what He has done. All that is asked of us is that we believe and receive.

Look to the Cross. Look at the amazing gift God gave you in the sacrifice of His Son. And realize that the same God, the same incredibly loving and amazingly generous Father who withheld nothing from you in the extravagant gift of His Son, would never withhold any of His gifts and blessings from you. Everything He is and everything He has are yours, because He loves you.

WHEN YOU UNDERSTAND THAT GOD HAS GIVEN EVERYTHING *FOR* YOU, IT IS EASY TO TRUST THAT HE HAS ALSO GIVEN EVERYTHING *TO* YOU!

–Robert Hotchkin

_____

_____

_____

Day 29

"THAT YOU, BEING ROOTED AND GROUNDED IN LOVE, MAY BE ABLE TO COMPREHEND WITH ALL THE SAINTS WHAT IS THE BREADTH AND LENGTH AND HEIGHT AND DEPTH, AND TO KNOW THE LOVE OF CHRIST WHICH SURPASSES KNOWLEDGE, THAT YOU MAY BE FILLED UP TO ALL THE FULLNESS OF GOD."
—EPHESIANS 3:17-19—

Paul desired the church at Ephesus to know the love of God so they could be flooded with all the fullness of God. Because God IS love, when we internalize His love we become filled with His fullness.

Our life's quest is to discover God's love and explore its fullness. When knowing the love of God becomes our first priority in life, we will see manifestations of His love and goodness every day and everywhere we look. Whatever you focus on, you empower. When you focus on His love, you empower that love to saturate you.

Although it will require all of eternity to discover the entirety of His love because it is so immense, you can begin your quest to explore it now. As you look for it, you will see the glory of His love each day of your life and it will transform you.

My prayer is that today you will sink your roots into His love and make it your firm foundation. May you be unshakable in your understanding of His unconditional perfect love, and may its power grow within from one glorious attribute of God to another. Today, make it your purpose to really know Christ and focus on His flawless love.

EXPLORE HIS LOVE TODAY — BE FILLED WITH ALL THE FULLNESS OF GOD!

–Patricia King

Day 30

"Nothing in all creation will ever be able
to separate us from the love of God that is revealed
in Christ Jesus our Lord."
—Romans 8:39 NLT—

There are few things certain in this world, few things you can really count on. But there is one – the love of God.

Think about the certainty of the promise in Romans 8:39. God is not only declaring the truth that He loves you, He is proclaiming for all eternity that you can boldly expect to be constantly in the midst of His amazing love. He promises that *nothing* in *all* creation can *ever* separate you from the love of God revealed in Christ. That is as ironclad certain as it gets!

No matter where you are. No matter what you are going through. No matter how things look or feel. No matter whether you're surrounded with support or seemingly all on your own. No matter what. There is nothing in the world – nothing in all of space or time, nothing that any person or devil can do – that can ever separate you from the love of God. You are always connected to His love. You are always in the midst of His love. You are always being perfectly, radically and abundantly loved. You can be certain of it!

Whatever you are facing. Whatever is going on in your life right now. Look to Jesus. Look to the Cross. Look to that revelation of God's perfect love that declares to all people for all time that there is nothing He would not do to prove His love to you and woo you back into the fullness of relationship with Him. Take a moment and remember that God loves you, and His love is always there for you – to strengthen you, comfort you, encourage you, and most of all remind you that you are precious to Him. You can be certain that all of His heart and all of His promises are for you – always!

GOD'S LOVE IS CERTAIN. YOU CAN COUNT ON IT IN EVERY SITUATION AND CIRCUMSTANCE!

–Robert Hotchkin

Day 31

"When they praised the Lord saying, 'He indeed is
good for His lovingkindness is everlasting,'
then the house, the house of the Lord,
was filled with a cloud, so that the priests could not
stand to minister because of the cloud,
for the glory of the Lord filled the house of God."
—2 Chronicles 5:13-14—

God is good, loving, and kind all the time. When you are certain God loves you, then you can be assured His goodness and kindness will follow you. In Psalm 23:6, the Scriptures declare, "Surely goodness and lovingkindness will follow me all the days of my life."

Did you catch that? It said, "ALL the days." That means EVERY day will be filled with the manifestation of God's goodness and kindness toward you and all that pertains to you. Read this unbelievable promise again and again until it really sinks in!

The priests mentioned above in 2 Chronicles 5 praised the Lord, declared His goodness and lovingkindness, and had quite the visitation from God! God likes it when we recognize the truth of His love and goodness, and declare it, because love is the first and last word in our relationship with Him.

Today declare His goodness and lovingkindness. Praise Him for His love! Look for the visitation of His goodness. Expect His kindness to manifest and it will! It really will!

> YOU ARE DEEPLY LOVED AND HIS GOODNESS
> AND LOVINGKINDNESS ARE WITH YOU!

–Patricia King

My Journal of Love Insights

My Journal of Love Insights

My Journal of Love Insights

My Journal of Love Insights

My Journal of Love Insights

My Journal of Love Insights

My Journal of Love Insights

My Journal of Love Insights

My Journal of Love Insights

My Journal of Love Insights

My Journal of Love Insights

My Journal of Love Insights

My Journal of Love Insights

My Journal of Love Insights

My Journal of Love Insights

My Journal of Love Insights

My Journal of Love Insights

My Journal of Love Insights

My Journal of Love Insights

My Journal of Love Insights

My Journal of Love Insights

My Journal of Love Insights

My Journal of Love Insights

My Journal of Love Insights

My Journal of Love Insights

My Journal of Love Insights

My Journal of Love Insights

My Journal of Love Insights

Appendix:
How to Have a Fruitful Devotional Time

by Patricia King

ESTABLISH A TIME TO BE ALONE WITH GOD EACH DAY.

I find that if I do not establish a time and discipline myself, then I keep putting it off. I will say things to myself like, "As soon as I finish these e-mails I will spend time with the Lord" or "as soon as I get dressed…" You probably know what I am talking about. It is easy to keep pushing it off and then discover at the end of the day that your hours were swallowed up, and you did not take the time to be with the Lord.

Personally, I like rising early to spend quality time with the Lord. I like giving the Lord the first and the best of my day. Once my quiet time is over, then I am ready to live a fruitful, blessed, and productive day. The psalmist said,

"IN THE MORNING, O LORD, YOU WILL HEAR MY VOICE; IN THE MORNING I WILL ORDER MY PRAYER TO YOU AND EAGERLY WATCH" — PSALM 5:3.

Others are not fresh in the morning but find other times in the day or evening easier for them. The issue is not when you spend time with God. The issue is making it a priority to spend time with God. Discipline yourself to spend time with Him.

Find a quiet place where you can be undistracted in your focus.

Moses pitched a tent a good distance away from the camp. He called it the tent of meeting. (See Exodus 33:7-9.) This was his appointed place to be with God. Every time he entered the tent, the pillar of cloud would descend, and God would speak to him face-to-face as a man speaks to a friend. Find a place for yourself that is void of distractions—an alone place where you meet with the Lord. This might be a room in your home or even a literal closet.

Jesus said, "When you pray, go into your inner room, close your door and pray to your Father who is in secret, and your Father who sees what is done in secret will reward you" (Matthew 6:6). Some versions use the term closet rather than inner room. Whether this literally means a particular room or closet or not, the room of the heart is to be opened to God and closed to distractions. The sacred time spent in this sacred place will then be rewarded openly.

On a mission field we served in years ago, our team lived in dormitory rooms with at least two or three others in the same room. Most people placed curtains around their bunks that produced a space boundary for themselves. They made that their "quiet place" where they met with God. Now that is a closet! (I have actually heard of individuals who literally pray in closets.)

When Ron and I lived in an inner city, I found my special place with God on a walking path at a local park. I would pray while power walking the track and then settle down in a nice spot on the grass under a tree to read my Bible, listen for God to speak, and journal. This was my place and my routine most days.

Sometimes I am on the road ministering, and I share a room with someone. In those cases, I usually go into the bathroom and lock the door or go for a prayer walk. There are times due to your lifestyle that you might need to get creative in establishing a place, but make it a priority. Establish your Sacred Place.

What do you do in a devotion time?

Everyone approaches God differently. Find out for yourself the best way to seek Him. The following are some things that can be included in a devotion time.

Commit yourself and your time to the Lord. Whatever you commit to Him becomes His to rule over and influence. Allow His grace and blessing to come upon you as you commit yourself and your time to the Lord.

Invite Holy Spirit to lead and guide you in your devotion time. Jesus called Holy Spirit your Helper. He will empower you and lead and guide you in your devotions if you invite Him.

Include praise and worship. Adoring and praising the Lord causes your focus on Him to be strengthened. Whatever you focus on, you empower. He is worthy of our praise and worship. Many like to soak with worship music and find this helpful in enhancing their relationship with the Lord.

Read the Scriptures. The Word of God is so powerful. You might want to use a Bible reading plan to help you read through the entire Bible in a year. Also allow the Spirit to lead you into portions. The Lord will speak to your heart through the Scriptures. The Bible is your handbook for life. You will gain wisdom, insight, and instruction through the Scriptures.

Pray. Prayer is simply talking to God. Share your heart and concerns with Him. When you pray, believe that you receive, and you shall have what you ask. (See Mark 11:24.) Always pray in faith. Praying in tongues is also powerful during devotion times. If you are not skilled in prayer, you might want to order my CD teaching set called "Increasing Your Prayer Power" and my book, "Tongues – God's Provision for Dynamic Growth and Supernatural Living." Get equipped and empowered.

Listen. Waiting quietly for the Lord to speak to your heart will allow Him the opportunity to pour into you. Often in prayer times believers talk and seldom listen. Take time to listen. Jesus only did the things He saw His Father do and only spoke what He heard His Father speak. Most of the time God will speak to you in His still small voice. For more training on hearing the voice of God, read my books "Eyes that See" and "Ears that Hear."

Journal. Journaling can include the penning of your love letters to God as you pour your heart out before Him, your prayer lists, special Bible promises and verses, visions, and prophetic insights or words that have been given you. Write in your journal the things God reveals to you. From time to time review your journal notes, and remember the things the Lord has spoken to you.

Decree. Decrees are declarations of God's Word. I love declaring the promises of God in my daily devotion times over my realms of influence. I use our Decree book to declare the Word over my life, family, ministries, businesses, partners, and staff. Decrees are powerful and a great way to focus on the Truth!

Make a list of things that distract. Sometimes in the midst of your devotion time you might receive some distracting thoughts such as, "Oh, I better remember to pay that bill later and e-mail a friend." Keep a small notepad available, and write those things down so you do not have to think on them again until after your devotion time is over.

Offer thanksgiving. At the end of your devotions, thank the Lord for the time He spent with you, and invite Him to continue to reveal His heart to yours throughout your day. Remain aware of His presence throughout the day.

About the Author Patricia King:

Patricia King's life message is that God loves us with an everlasting love. She has gone around the world sharing the love of God in word and power. More than 30 years ago, Patricia gave her life fully to Jesus Christ and the advancement of His Kingdom in the earth. She is a respected minister of the gospel, recognized prophet, inventive entrepreneur, successful businesswoman, accomplished itinerant speaker, author, media innovator, and host of Everlasting Love TV.

Her desire is to see everyone come to know Jesus through an experience of His incredible love for them, and to help bring believers into a deeper and more intimate relationship with the Lord so the reality of His glorious presence and supernatural power becomes an everyday occurrence in their lives. She lives in Maricopa, Arizona, with her husband Ron, who has been an amazing expression of God's love to her for more than three decades!

ABOUT THE AUTHOR ROBERT HOTCHKIN:

Robert Hotchkin is a "spiritual son" of Patricia King. He has served in XP Ministries with Patricia and her husband Ron since 2004. In November of 2002, Rob was splitting wood in the mountains when he was radically saved and forever changed by the first of many encounters with the love of Jesus. He went from being a mocker and persecutor of Christians to a passionate lover of Christ.

That passion for the Lord marks his ministry, and it is truly contagious. Rob travels the world, ministering with strong faith, releasing revelation, prophetic decrees, healings, miracles, and the love of God. He is a carrier of the glory and a sparker of revival fires. People have been healed, refreshed, set free, and empowered through his life. His great desire is that every person, city, nation and region would know that God is good and that He really, really loves them!

SUGGESTED RESOURCES

Decree the Word!

Decree a thing and it shall be established. Job 22:28

The Word of God is powerful, and it accomplishes everything that it is sent to do. The expanded **Decree, Third Edition** helps believers activate the power of the Word in key areas of their lives, including health, provision, love, victory, wisdom, family, business, blessing, favor and others. New Derees in this edition are "Great Grace," "Rejuvenation," "12 Decrees for Your Nation," and "I Am Supernatural in Christ."

An Invitation to Spend Time with God

Sacred Time – Sacred Place, a Journal

This beautiful imitation leather journal has valuable tools for developing a rich devotional life. It includes practical guidelines to help you have a fruitful devotional time with Jesus, a plan to read the Bible in one year, and plenty of lined pages with a Bible Scripture at the bottom. Packaged in a gift box.

SUGGESTED RESOURCES

Soak and Listen to this Powerful Message!

Ultimate Passion CD by Patricia King and Steve Swanson. Patricia shares a powerful message on the Cross. She not only teaches on the Cross, but prophesies from God's perspective the message of His love for each and every one of us. Steve flows in powerful worship anointing, adding to the unfolding of this amazing revelation.

Experience the Father's Love.

The Power of His Love by Robert Hotchkin. There is a power that comes from knowing the Father's love for us. Healings happen. Deliverances happen. Miracles happen. The Kingdom happens. Robert shares aspects of his testimony along with revelation from Scripture that will release you into a new experience of God's love for you.

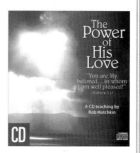

These and many other impacting and inspiring resources are available at the "store" at:
XPMINISTRIES.COM

Additional copies of this book and other resources
from Patricia King and Robert Hotchkin,
as well as other XP Publishing books,
are available at XPministries.com

Wholesale prices for stores and ministries

Please contact:
usaresource@xpministries.com.

In Canada, please contact:
resource@xpministries.com.

XP Publishing books are also available to
wholesale and retail stores through
anchordistributors.com

A MINSTRY OF XP MINISTRIES